SIMPLE
GOLF

BACK TO BASICS

Box Design: Hinkler Design Studio

Creative Director: Sam Grimmer

Editor: Hinkler Books

Book Design: Sam Grimmer

Photography: Ned Meldrum

Special thanks to Riversdale Golf Club

for their help and assistance.

First published in 2005
by Hinkler Books Pty Ltd
17-23 Redwood Drive
Dingley Victoria 3172 Australia
www.hinklerbooks.com

Printed and bound in China

ISBN   1 7415 7322 X

CONTENTS

INTRODUCTION

Enjoyment of golf, regardless of the level you play at, is primarily based on how closely you play to your level of ability. The better you play, the more enjoyment you get from the game. This book has something in it for everyone who plays the game – whether you are an absolute beginner, part-time social player or avid fanatic. *Simply Golf – Back to Basics* covers the essential elements of the game you need to understand if you are to play to your potential and receive ultimate enjoyment from the game.

Golfers are motivated by good shots, the thrill of competition, and the challenge of improving their current skill level. I am a firm believer that we are all driven by one of two instincts: either to avoid pain, or to gain pleasure. Therefore, golfers will practise for one of these two reasons.

Tour professionals may practise 3 ft putts for hours on end because they are trying to avoid the pain of missing short putts in competition, which is very costly. This is practising to avoid pain, and it is my belief that eventually their brain will steer them away from this high level of practice, because one of its primary functions is to avoid pain.

But what if the same golfer interpreted 3 ft putts as fun? They would still practise for hours on end for the sheer enjoyment of putting the ball in the hole from this distance. I know this golfer is more likely to make critical 3 ft putts in competition, and continue to do so for years on end, because their motivation for practice is based on the enjoyment and pleasure of succeeding at this particular skill.

As long as a golfer is motivated to practise by the enjoyment and the thrill of playing the game and succeeding at new challenges, the game of golf and all of its intricate skills will offer a lifetime of reward and pleasure. If, however, you find yourself practising out of fear of failure and the frustration of not living up to your expectations, it is my belief

that the enjoyment of golf and the benefits that you can receive from the game will eventually diminish. Your brain will say 'enough is enough!' and you'll find something else to enjoy.

My approach to teaching golf is a holistic one. Every sport that is played well requires the essential knowledge of the following four basic factors:

- TECHNIQUE
- MENTAL SKILLS
- STRATEGY
- PHYSICAL ABILITY

TECHNIQUE

There is not one golf swing for everybody, but I do believe there is a golf swing that fits each of us as individuals. This swing is right for you because it takes into account your body type, flexibility, age, available practice time, inherent athletic ability and your commitment to the game. A sound knowledge of the essential basics of golf technique is required in the three main areas of:

- THE FULL SWING • THE SHORT GAME
- PUTTING

In every round of golf you play, you will most likely encounter the need to play specific shots in one of the eleven shot categories of:

- DRIVER • FAIRWAY WOODS/METALS
- LONG IRONS • MID IRONS • SHORT IRONS
- PITCHING • BUNKER PLAY • CHIPPING
- LONG PUTTS • MID-RANGE PUTTS
- SHORT PUTTS

This may sound overwhelming, but I assure you that the basics from all the different shot categories don't vary that much. It is, however, important to understand the differences and basics required to help maximise your golf enjoyment.

MENTAL SKILLS

It is not possible to play golf consistently well without sound mental skills. However, every person playing the game has the basis of good mental skills for golf. They are simply the refined mental skills that we already possess and use that help us function through everyday life. You need to use and improve the three mental Cs:

- COMMITMENT (dedication to practice, ability to cope with disappointment)
- CONCENTRATION (the ability to think exclusively about the task at hand)
- CONFIDENCE (the direct result of experience and preparation and the ability to recall positive experiences)

Enhance the three Cs and you will have all the mental skills required to play golf to your full potential. Just like the golf swing itself, however, if your mental skills are not up to standard, there are drills and exercises in this book and DVD that can be practised to help you improve.

STRATEGY

Strategy is the ability to play the game. It can be described as 'course management', made up of shot, target and club selection. Part of the strategy of golf includes how to practise based on your assessment and goals.

Like chess, golf is a game of strategy. It takes a lifetime to learn all the moves and tactics and yet only a very short time to master the basics of how the game is played. A golfer who can think their way around the course and is well prepared for the game will always enjoy playing.

In the *Simply Golf – Back to Basics* section on Strategy you will find advice on the important elements of strategy, including the 'one shot at a time' attitude and the tactical approach of 'traffic light golf'.

PHYSICAL ABILITY

Physical conditioning is very important. Your technique can only function as well as your body will allow. I have seen many swings change for the better in golf through improved physical condition, often without the golfer being consciously aware of the change. You can't hit the ball 300 yards like a tour professional unless your physical attributes allow it. Everybody can improve their physical condition for golf. The important physical areas are: flexibility, coordination, diet, strength (particularly core strength), aerobic condition, rhythm and balance.

When I say everyone can improve upon their current condition, I am not suggesting we can all be like the world's best tour pros. However, we can all get into better shape, no matter what our age.

It is not the scope of this book to cover in any great detail all of the areas of physical conditioning for golf. However, you might like to refer to the 10 essential stretches in the Physical Preparation section later on.

FOR BETTER OR WORSE, HOW DO THINGS CHANGE?

Golf swings change for one of three reasons:

- A concept change: we deliberately make a move or position change based on new information.
- A physical change: our body is different because of some sort of activity, injury or the natural process of ageing.
- A reflex change: our coordination is reacting at a subconscious level, generally as a result of recent shots and swings. An example is that a golfer may start coming over the top in their swing (swinging the club from out to the side to across the swing line) in reaction to the last few shots finishing right of the target.

From my experience, there are several categories of golfers.

The Obsessive Perfectionist is the golfer who is passionate about golf technique. This golfer thinks that the key to golf is a perfect technique and when they achieve that, they will be able to play. They read and try all the magazine tips available, books and videos, listen to their friends' advice, and spend a fortune on lessons. Rarely does the perfectionist enjoy their game, because the reality is that golf can't be perfected, so they can never live up to their own unrealistic expectations.

The second type, the opposite to the Obsessive Perfectionist, is the 'I Don't Want to Know Anything' type. This golfer just wants to hit the ball and not think about anything confusing like technique. This so-called simple approach rarely works because when something goes wrong, and it invariably does, there is nowhere to turn to solve the problem.

Then there is the Equipment Addict. This golfer sees the answer in a new driver, putter, set of clubs or even shoes and a bag almost every time they play. Well, I am sure these golfers have no trouble finding a

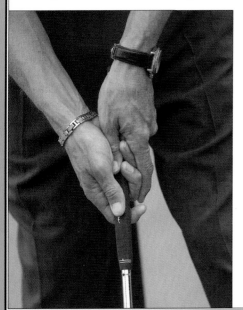

retailer to accommodate them! Unfortunately, the satisfaction achieved is short-lived; when the new driver no longer hits it 20 yards further and straighter, it's back to the Pro shop for the latest and greatest model.

Then there are golfers who think that the game is all mind-power: '50% of golf is 100% mind-power', they declare. That's right up there with the classic saying '90% of short putts don't go in'. If you believe this type, you will see that they're 'just about' to play golf well. (Funny how that day never quite seems to arrive.)

And then there is the golfer who has the answer in a new physical conditioning program: yoga, pilates, tai chi, aerobics. There's nothing wrong with doing any of these to improve your fitness, but alone they won't improve your golf!

Do any of these characters above sound like you? Maybe there's a bit of each of them in you. Go on, admit it, and start improving your golf!

In fact, there is no one element of the four training factors that is the whole secret to better golf. They all play an important role. The key is balance and awareness of your strengths and weaknesses. A general rule is if you have enough knowledge of the basics to maintain the things you are good at and improve the areas where you have potential, then the game of golf will be one of constant enjoyment. Of course, there will be highs and lows from round to round, but that is the beauty of golf. The good shots bring us back the next time and the bad shots help us to define the good ones.

HOW DO WE LEARN?

THE IMPROVEMENT CYCLE

This is a time- and result-proven method for improving any skill. In golf there are two types of learning cycles. One I call the improvement cycle, the other the reactive cycle. The improvement cycle has three phases and, as the name suggests, the phases repeat over and over.

The first of the three phases is for the

golfer to be able to make an objective assessment of where their current particular skill level is. If it is a technique skill that is assessed, this can be done by video, computer analysis, and visual observation by an instructor or use of mirrors or training aids. If it is a playing skill that is being assessed, this is best done by the use of skills tests on the practice range, course playing statistics and self or an instructor's observation.

The next step based on the assessment is to set a realistic goal of where they would like that skill level to be in a certain time frame.

The final phase is to set some specific tasks (drills, exercises, skills tests, practice programs) to achieve that goal. The cycle then begins again with reassessment, setting goals and implementing a practice plan.

I prefer and often use a three-week improvement cycle (21 days). If you were to practise a particular skill correctly for 21 days, there is a very good chance that skill will be ingrained. There is no conclusive evidence to prove that 21 days is how long it takes humans to adapt to change, even though many sports coaches swear by this. But I do know that every person I have recommended work through a 21-day improvement cycle has done just that: improved. In theory, advanced and dedicated golfers could do a three-week improvement cycle 17 times per year, with one week off for good behaviour.

THE REACTIVE CYCLE

Yet I know people who practise golf every day of the year and seem only to make marginal improvements, if at all. If they were to use the improvement cycle and practise only for half the year, I am sure they would see improvement beyond their imagination. These golfers practise the game using the reactive cycle. The reactive cycle is also cyclical, but, unfortunately, what most golfers keep returning to are old bad habits that limit their ability to make any real improvements. Golfers in a reactive cycle

keep repeating the same mistakes whilst expecting a different result.

The reactive cycle works like this. First, the golfer hits a shot and if the ball slices to the right, on the very next shot they try something in their swing, either from a book, magazine, lesson, tip from a friend etc. to not slice the ball. This tip may work for a few shots until the ball starts going low and to the left. The cycle begins again with the golfer reacting to this by trying to correct the shot. I see golfers every day practising this way. Consequently, they become frustrated and disenchanted with the game and fail to achieve what they are really capable of.

DRILLS

WHAT IS A DRILL AND WHY DO DRILLS WORK?

Drills are a training exercise that emphasise a particular area of the skill that needs change. Drills work because they enable the golfer to isolate that area and focus on the correct motor pattern change without influence from the original one, and without the interruption of worrying about ball flight, contact or another area of the skill. I use a three-step approach to using drills that incorporates introducing the new pattern into the entire motion of the skill:

- Step one: do one or more of the drills to ingrain the awareness of how it feels and functions.
- Step two: incorporate the feel into a practice swing.
- Step three: hit a golf ball with no other thought than the awareness of the drill blending into the swing. It is very important not to be concerned at all by ball flight when you are working with drills to modify technique.

Quite simply, you can improve your skills by using the improvement cycle to:

- Identify problems.
- Find drills and practise activities that target

the problem.
- Perform the drill or activity long enough and with the correct process to cause improvement.

There are two types of drills:

- Practising the mechanics: where different sorts of training aids and drills may be used. When practising mechanics, you should evaluate your performance by whether you achieve the particular move or sequence in the technique you are practising. Never evaluate success or failure by where the ball goes. It is a good idea to practise mechanics in a net if you have trouble with not isolating your thoughts from ball flight.

- Practising golf: activities where the golfer develops routines and techniques that they can take to the course without the need for, or use of, outside aids. Practising golf is all about scoring and where the ball goes. When practising golf only evaluate your success or failure by where the ball goes, not by how you swing the club or how it feels.

TAKING YOUR PRACTICE GAME TO THE COURSE

One of the most commonly misunderstood areas of golf lies in the question 'how we can practise well and then go out on the course and play poorly?'. The answer is in understanding the difference between practising golf and practising technique. Just having a good swing or putting stroke doesn't guarantee that we will score well when we go to the course. The golfer needs to have good mental, strategic and physical basics to be able to convert practice ability into quality play.

The most valuable skill a golfer must have is to develop a sound technique with all their clubs and shots. This is the major step towards playing with confidence. A balanced practice program, which includes the shots required in proportion to what is needed on the golf course, is essential to consistent performance. Approximately 60% of all shots are in the short game category. Therefore, it would make good sense if approximately 60% of your practice time was spent on the short-game shots. The three-hour practice program drill is a very effective approach for managing your practice program effectively.

THREE-HOUR PRACTICE PROGRAM

For every three hours that you practise, attempt to divide your practice time so that you would spend one hour on the full swing, one hour on chipping, pitching and bunker play and one hour on putting. The one hour of full swing should be divided proportionally between driving, fairway metals, long, mid and short irons. And the one hour of putting between long, mid and short range putts. If you practise consistently with this balanced approach, there will be no shot you are confronted with on the course that you will not have confidence in playing as a result of your recent practice.

If you are standing over a shot and you can't remember the last time you played that shot in practice with success, it is highly unlikely that you will have the necessary confidence to pull that shot off to your satisfaction on the course.

The key to success is the balanced approach to practice by following the above guidelines of the three-hour practice program.

Physical Preparation

Ten essential stretches for golf

Most of the world's best golfers warm up and stretch their muscles before they hit balls. So when you see a tournament golfer hitting balls on the practice range before a round, they have already warmed up their body.

Most club and social golfers don't even hit balls before they play. Most probably they have come straight from the office or school and they are so keen to play that they go to the first tee without any sort of warm up. This is not only the worst thing you can do for your game, it may expose you to the possibility of a soft tissue injury.

The ten essential stretches for golf are all specific to the swing. They will greatly reduce the chance of injury and will help with the overall function and performance of your golf swing.

Five minutes before and five minutes after you play is all that is required to do the ten essential stretches. Your body will thank you and your golf game will reap the rewards.

What you will find after only a few days of stretching is that the golf swing will seem easier and more coordinated and this will help tremendously with your consistency and overall confidence.

Warm up for 30 seconds with some pivot rotation. Ideally a brisk walk, some star jumps or a few minutes on an exercise bike.

Pivot rotation

Prepares your body for the pivoting motion of the golf swing.

1 Place a club behind your back and through your elbows as shown.

2 Rotate around the axis of your back to the right and then left a few times to loosen up your back and hip muscles.

3 Take your golf posture and rotate to the right in a fashion as close as you can to your actual golf swing. Hold this position for 10 seconds and then rotate through to your finish position and hold that for ten seconds.

4 Repeat three times on each side.

Wrist extension/flexion

Prepares your wrists for the load and jarring that can occur whilst hitting balls and releases built up tension.

1 Extend an arm out in front of you as shown. With the opposite hand, gently pull back on your fingers until you feel a stretch in the forearm and wrist. Hold this position for 10 seconds.

2 Pull down on your hand until you feel a stretch in the back of your wrist and forearm. Once again hold this for 10 seconds and repeat three times.

3 Change arms between each pair of stretches.

FOREARMS

Prepares muscles and tendons in the forearms that are under stress from the extension and rotation of the swing.

1 Extend your arms in front of you and turn your palms out as shown.

2 Place one hand over the other and interlock fingers.

3 Extend the back of your top hand towards your face until you feel a stretch in the other arm along the top of your forearm. Hold this for 10 seconds and then alternate arms.

4 Repeat three times.

SHOULDER EXTENSION

Prepares your shoulders for the extension required during the back-swing and follow through.

1 Extend an arm across in front of your body and clasp back and below the elbow with the opposite arm as shown.

2 Pull your arm across until you feel a stretch through the back of the shoulder of the extended arm.

3 Hold this stretch for 10 seconds and then alternate arms. Repeat three times.

4 Try turning your head the opposite way to your extended arm so you feel a stretch through your neck as well as your shoulder. This is particularly good for the back swing and your ability to swing to the top without too much head rotation.

SIDE OF NECK AND TOP OF SHOULDERS

Prepares the neck muscles for the bracing of your target side at and through impact. This area is where many golfers become tense through mental stress.

1 Standing with good posture, tilt your head to the side and clasp it as shown.

2 Pull across from the side of your head and extend the fingers of the hanging arm down toward the ground. You will feel a stretch from your ear, the side of your neck and across the top of your shoulder.

3 Hold this stretch for 10 seconds, alternate sides and repeat three times.

PHYSICAL PREPARATION

BACK OF UPPER ARMS AND SIDE OF UPPER BACK

Prepares the arms and back for the leverage created and required during the down-swing to develop power.

1 Put an arm behind your head and touch the opposite shoulder with your fingers.

2 Clasp the back of your elbow with the opposite hand and pull across gently until you feel a stretch under the arm.

3 Hold for 5 seconds and then lean to the side. You should now feel the stretch extend down through the side of your upper back (these muscles under the arm and back are the muscles that are activated to create leverage in the down-swing).

4 Alternate sides and repeat three times.

BUTTOCK MUSCLES

The big muscles in your backside, called gluteals, are major contributors to the power created in the pivot. They can also become tight as a result of the demands of the swing and the walking required.

1 Sit on a bench or seat and cross a leg as shown.

2 Clasp your hands together in front of the opposite knee and pull forward. You will feel the stretch through your buttocks and hip of the crossed leg.

3 Hold this stretch for 10 seconds, alternate legs and repeat three times.

BACK OF UPPER LEGS

Prepares the hamstrings for the demands of the swing particularly the role they play in stabilising posture. Hamstrings can become tight with walking up and down slopes on the course.

1 Extend a leg and rest your heel on a bench or chair as shown.

2 Maintain good posture in your back as you push down through the heel on the bench. You will feel a stretch through the back of the leg.

3 Hold this stretch for 10 seconds, alternate legs and repeat three times.

FRONT OF HIPS

Prepares the hip flexors for the demands of the swing, particularly the role they play in stabilising posture and pivot.

1 Kneel on one leg, with your opposite leg not quite fully extended in front. Support yourself with a bench or chair while keeping your body upright and in a good posture.

2 Rock forward until you feel the stretch through the front of your hip.

3 Hold for 10 seconds, change legs and repeat three times.

SIDE STRETCH

Prepares the muscles in the side of your lower back that play a major role in the rotation range of the pivot motion.

1 Stand side-on to a wall or a tree with an arm fully extended, palm against the wall.

2 Cross the leg nearest the wall over the opposite leg.

3 Sink your hip nearest the wall towards it and take most of your weight on that leg. You will feel the stretch in the side of your lower back and the outside of your hip. Hold this stretch for 10 seconds, alternate sides and repeat three times.

Back to Basics: Technique

Golf technique can be categorised into four major categories. They are relevant to all shots, from putting through to driving.

- SET-UP: includes the grip, stance, ball position and alignment.

- PIVOT: includes every part of the body that pivots on an axis in the swing: the head, the shoulders, the hips, the legs and foot action.

- PLANE AND POSITION: includes the function of the arms, elbows and wrists and their influence on the shaft and club-head.

- DYNAMICS: rhythm, timing, balance and tempo.

A good set-up is the starting point for all golf techniques. After a correct set-up, the pivot action of the body is the nucleus of the golf swing. Plane and position, which is the action of the arms and path and position of the shaft and club-head throughout the swing, is primarily a response to the pivot motion. Governing and linking set-up pivot and plane and position together are other dynamics of rhythm, timing balance and tempo. Put simply, set-up influences pivot, pivot influences plane and position and the dynamics of balance, rhythm and timing control precision and consistency of the technique.

POSTURE

It is absolutely essential to have good posture in the set-up. The five-step posture drill is the most effective and simple to use of all the posture drills I have seen and used.

THE POSTURE ROUTINE

1 Place a club on the ground pointing to the target to use as an alignment guide. Stand with your feet shoulder-width apart while facing parallel to the golf club on the ground. Rest a club you are going to hit with against your hips as shown. Turn your palms out and extend your arms down, to position your posture in the correct and most natural shape for your back. This occurs as a result of moving your shoulders back and down.

2 While maintaining the shape of your back, bend forward from the top of your legs until your upper body is at the approximate angle that you will need to hit the ball.

3 Now unlock your knees and balance your weight evenly from left to right foot and through the balls of your feet.

4 Move your left hip toward the target and your right shoulder away whilst maintaining parallel alignment. The correct amount of upper body tilt can be checked in a mirror. The outside of your left leg and upper body should form a straight line and there should be a visible angle between your right leg and right side. This position allows your right hand to fit below the left on the grip without any twist or manipulation of your back and shoulders.

5 Let your arms fall forward into their most natural hanging position and move them into a position that you can grip the club. You will now be the correct distance from the ball.

Grip

The golf grip is our only connection with the club. It plays the most important role of clubface awareness and the ability to consistently square the clubface at impact, which results in accurate shot making. There are certain essential elements of a good golf grip, but as with much of golf there are allowances for individual preferences. The key is consistency – the ability to put your hands on the club the same way every time. This will happen when you understand what a good grip is, how to practise it, and then develop a grip routine that enables you to put your hands on the club the same way every time.

TRAINING GRIP

I encourage all of my students to have a practice club with a training grip on it. I have had one since I first played golf and have always had a good grip. Every one of my students who uses a training grip in practice grips the club consistently well.

THE GRIP ROUTINE

1 With the clubface aimed at the target, pinch the grip cap between your thumb and index finger as shown.

2 Now place your left hand to the side of the grip and make contact from the second joint of your index finger to just above the root of your index finger.

3 Wrap your hand around the grip. Your left hand is now in perfect position.

4 Pick up the club and hold it out in front of you with the toe of the club pointing skyward.

5 Now place your right hand to the side of the grip in the same manner as the left and wrap your hand around. The little finger of your right hand will need to interlock with the left index finger or overlap. You should feel the life line of your right hand fitting snugly against your left thumb and your overall grip pressure should give you a sense of control and firmness, but without tension in your arms that will lead to restricting the motion of the swing.

Practise this grip routine regularly with your training grip and develop a consistent routine for gripping the club in practice and play. You will benefit with consistent and accurate shots in your play.

STANCE AND BALL POSITION

There are three different stance widths and ball positions you will need to understand for the full-swing categories of woods, fairway shots and short irons. Some methods that are described in books are in theory simpler, by advocating only one ball position and stance for all shots. This sounds enticing and uncomplicated, but in fact it makes the golf swing itself more complicated.

The fact is that we are trying to do different things with the three shot categories. With woods we are trying to make contact with the ball at the bottom of our swing, which is always directly opposite the left shoulder joint. This creates minimum back spin so when the ball hits the ground it will run, maximising distance.

With fairway shots, we want to catch the ball just before the bottom of the swing creating a slightly steeper angle of attack, resulting in increased back spin and a shot that will stop when it lands on the target area. To achieve this, you need to play the ball back 5cm to 7.5cm toward the middle of your stance so you meet the ball before the bottom of the swing, which is always opposite the left shoulder joint.

With short irons we play the ball in the middle of the stance creating quite a steep angle of attack, catching the ball approximately 10cm (4 to 5 inches) before the bottom of the swing and consequently creating maximum back spin.

If you were to try and achieve these different angles of attack from the same stance and ball position, it would mean the swing itself would have to be manipulated and timed differently for each individual shot. So what starts out as being simple in theory with only one stance and ball position required actually becomes quite complex.

If you learn and use the three-ball position system you will actually be able to make what feels like the same swing at all shots. This leads to more consistency and greater enjoyment of the game.

THE STANCE

For all full swing shots I prefer and use a parallel alignment of the feet to the target line. This promotes a very good perspective of the path that you want to swing the club through. As for the feet, both should be splayed out with the left foot turned out at approximately 30°. This allows you to turn your hips through to face on to the target with your left foot still flat on the ground. If your left foot is not turned out to 30° you will have to roll over at the ankle onto the side of the foot or have the foot spin around through the swing which, of course, is then unbalanced. The right foot only needs to be turned out about 10°. This encourages turn rather than slide but also creates resistance as you approach the top of the back swing. Resistance or stretch sets up the stretch reflex that is crucial in a good transition from back swing to down-swing.

I recommend three different width stances for the three shot categories. This is not essential but it helps define the shot categories and encourages the appropriate swing feel for each shot.

WOODS: I like the stance to be wide enough that the insides of your feet are in line with the outside of your shoulders. This provides a solid and stable base, which is important to maintain balance and stability throughout the swing with the longer shafted clubs.

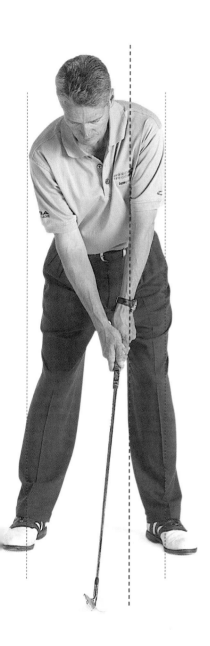

FAIRWAY SHOTS: I recommend a width stance that is slightly narrower than the woods. Your laces should now line up with the outside of your shoulders. This allows for a little more freedom in your hip pivot, but still provides the necessary stable base.

SHORT IRONS: I like a width stance that has the outside of your feet lining up with the outside of your shoulders. This allows for yet more freedom with your pivot and encourages a free and balanced motion.

FULL SWING: WOODS

THE SEVEN-STEP SWING

The golf swing is always a blend of the four major attributes listed above. The set-up influences pivot, pivot influences plane and position, and the dynamics of rhythm, timing, balance and tempo have an overall significance with the power, consistency and control of the swing.

A good golf swing will be rhythmical and fluent with a continual and even-paced motion from start to finish. I have found through my years of playing and teaching that the most effective way of learning the swing is to break it down into the seven-step swing. These steps are all static, but by positioning the body and club in these positions you can develop an awareness of what your body and arms have to do to achieve these positions. Then integrate that feel into a practice swing and finally hit a shot with that swing. Using this process of developing technique creates awareness and feel and the routine is very close to the routine of playing. The ultimate goal is to trust your practice swing and repeat it with the ball in play. You don't want to rethink or consciously manipulate the club during the swing. You will always repeat the last thing you did (the practice swing). Therefore, your goal is to develop a preparation routine that you can trust on the course. This must start on the practice fairway.

PRACTICE ROUTINE

Always start in the correct set-up position. There is no value in doing a drill from the incorrect set-up. If you do, when it comes to trying to integrate the drill into the actual swing, your coordination will fail.

From the set-up, position the club and your body in one of the next six positions. Hold this position for a few seconds, check it with a mirror and then close your eyes and tune in to what everything feels like. Return to the set-up position and then in a practice swing, focus on swinging through that position with one continual motion. (This often works best with your eyes closed as well). Note: every move in the golf swing, no matter how subtle, starts with the pivot. The 'inside moves the outside'.

1

Set-up: set-up to the ball as shown in the posture, stance and ball position drill.

2

Take-away: the triangle of your arms and shoulders start back in one united movement, then your wrists and right elbow activate with the right wrist hinging and the elbow folding. The club should be on plane by the time your hands are at waist height. On plane is demonstrated by the butt end of the club pointing at the inside quarter of the ball.

3

Top position: your arms and body are in motion by this stage. The feeling from step 2 is one of connection and harmony with a smooth and united move to the top of the back-swing. If timed correctly, the club, arms and shoulders will arrive at the top at the same time. Your weight should be approximately two-thirds over the right knee. From face on, the right elbow should fold to an angle of 90°, which will ensure the hands stay to the right of your head. From behind, the clubface is square if the leading edge is parallel to the left forearm.

4

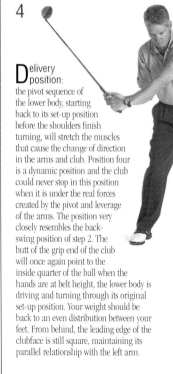

Delivery position:
the pivot sequence of the lower body, starting back to its set-up position before the shoulders finish turning, will stretch the muscles that cause the change of direction in the arms and club. Position four is a dynamic position and the club could never stop in this position when it is under the real forces created by the pivot and leverage of the arms. The position very closely resembles the back-swing position of step 2. The butt of the grip end of the club will once again point to the inside quarter of the ball when the hands are at belt height, the lower body is driving and turning through its original set-up position. Your weight should be back to an even distribution between your feet. From behind, the leading edge of the clubface is still square, maintaining its parallel relationship with the left arm.

5

Impact: from face on, the club shaft will be in line with your left arm and the butt of the club pointing at the left hip. The back of the left wrist will be flat and the right wrist and elbow have some angle left. From behind, the shoulders are back to their set-up position, the hips slightly open to the target line and the shaft will form a straight line with the right forearm. The clubface is square to the target. Approximately two-thirds of your weight will now be over your left knee. It is important to always be aware that these are static positions only in the seven step drill. In the actual swing they are positions that are dynamic and passed through with a continuous flowing motion.

6

Follow through: the ball is on its way but it's also important what happens in the swing after the hit. The follow-through position, balance and coordination are always good indicators of how good the preceding swing was. Many good players only think about one simple key thought, like the follow-through or finish position knowing that their coordination will do whatever is necessary to find the easiest pathway to that position. From face on, the follow-through position is almost a mirror image of the take-away and delivery positions. The butt of the club will point to where the ball was when the hands are just above waist height. The left elbow has started to fold. Your chest and belt buckle should still be turning, but facing the target at this position. The right heel is off the ground and the right knee is facing the target. Most importantly your head should be rotating with your pivot, no attempt should ever be made to keep your head down or still. It is still centred in the follow-through position, but turning with the motion of the swing.

7

The finish: the club should finish in a close-to-horizontal position behind your eye line. The right side has completely rotated around the left side. The right shoulder has now rotated past the left shoulder and is now over the top of the left foot. There is a complete release of the head position so that there is no arch in the back that can cause unnecessary back injury. Your body should be vertically balanced over your left foot, with the right foot up on the tip of the toe with all energy released. You should be in a relaxed and balanced position so you can enjoy watching the flight of the ball.

Woods Overview

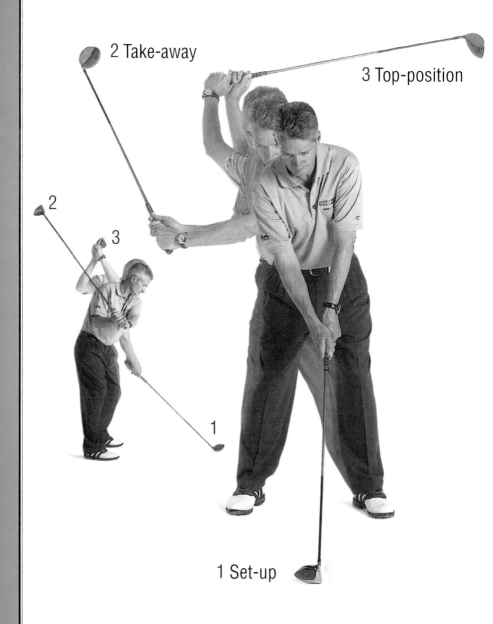

2 Take-away

3 Top-position

2

3

1

1 Set-up

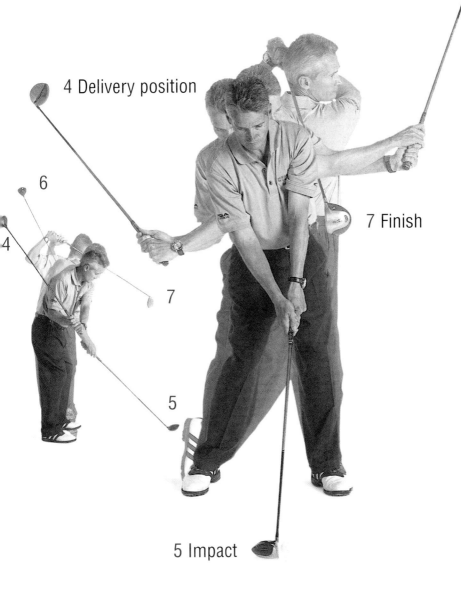

6 Follow through

4 Delivery position

6

4

7 Finish

7

5

5 Impact

Full Swing: Fairway Shots

The seven steps are the same for the full swing categories of woods, fairway shots and short irons. There are differences, however, that are the result of the variation in the set up or the different length of the clubs. These differences are pointed out but are best understood visually by observing the swing sequences.

Take your stance, posture and ball position as described in the set-up section for fairway shots.

The key thought for all full shots is to feel that you are making the same swing from a rhythm, timing and tempo execution. The clubs are designed to hit the ball further or shorter, so you don't need to change your swing. Having said that, the swing will look different from a short to a long club, because the length of the club varies and we stand closer or further away from the ball depending on the club. This means the swing plane will be flatter for the longer clubs and more upright for the shorter clubs. The length of the swing will vary from shorter to longer, again as a result of the length of the club. The longer clubs, like the driver for instance, create more leverage and produce a longer back swing than the wedge, which has a shorter shaft and will create a shorter back swing. The most common fault with the longer clubs is to try to swing harder in an effort to hit it further. This often results in miss hits and ruins your timing and tempo.

To maintain the feel of the same swing I recommend practising by alternating regularly between short, mid and driver shots with the goal of finding a good rhythm and tempo with the shorter clubs and maintaining that whilst hitting the longer clubs. Avoid hitting any more than five to ten balls consecutively with a driver or fairway metal. As well as having little to do with the context of what is required on the course, it almost always leads to a tempo and rhythm problem as it is very difficult to maintain a smooth and balanced swing.

1

2

3

4

5

6

7

Fairway Shots Overview

2 Take-away

3 Top-position

3

2

1

1 Set-up

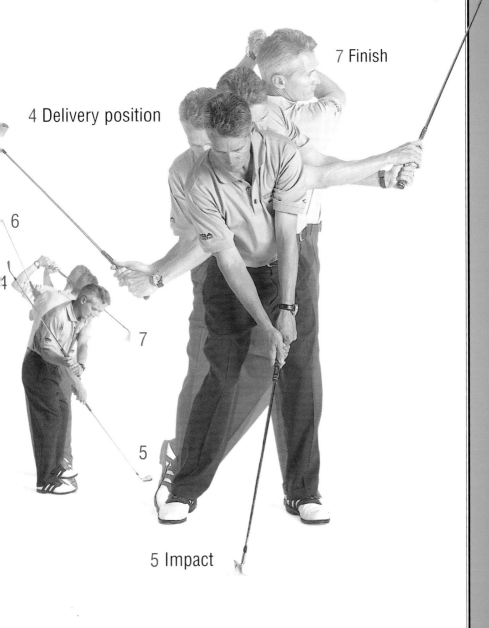

6 Follow through

7 Finish

4 Delivery position

6

4

7

5

5 Impact

FULL SWING: SHORT IRONS

THE SHORT GAME

The long game is often described as the most exciting part of golf while putting is seen as the game within a game. Pitching and chipping are often simply forgotten. Yet it is nonetheless a critical part of your game.

Statistically, the world's best golfers average around 13 greens in regulation per 18-hole round. And yet the leading scoring averages are around 3 under par. The world's best are averaging 28 to 29 putts per round. The easiest way to achieve this is to consistently hit your short-game shots close to the hole. The world's best will get up and down from the fairway and green surround around 70% of the time and approximately 60% of the time from greenside bunkers. This fact, combined with making about 3 to 4 birdies per round on average, accounts for the sub 30 putts per round average.

Too often, golfers, when faced with a chip or a putt, simply 'hit and hope' without giving the shot the thought it merits. The aim of these shots should always be to get the ball as close as possible to the hole (preferably in), always landing on the green.

Your shot should be targeted at a pre-determined spot on the green and be thought through to allow for the ball to run to the cup. Inherent in this consideration should be the resolve that the ball needs to land on a flat surface and should therefore be steered away from slopes of any kind.

'Feel' plays an important role, and coupled with this is the need for a consistent golf stroke as well as knowledge about club selection. However, the club of choice for many off-the-green shots, especially where the ball is only just off-the-green or lies in a depression or on bare earth, is the putter.

Naturally, it depends on the actual condition of the course and the grass, but the putter will frequently produce an acceptable shot given the earlier objective of getting the ball as close as possible to the hole. Whichever way you decide to go during competition, your practice should include using your putter in ways and situations other than for 'normal' putting.

Different clubs have different loft angles, and the same stroke with a different club produces different distances. Therefore, you should maintain your technique and allow the differences in clubface to accomplish the objective. I recommend that, wherever possible, you let the club do the work rather than altering your swing to accommodate the changes in lie or position.

1

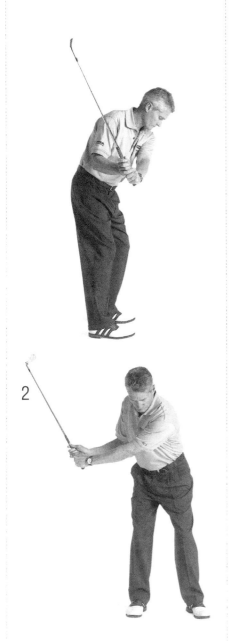

2

3

4

5

6

7

Short Irons Overview

2 Take-away

3 Top-position

3

2

1

1 Set-up

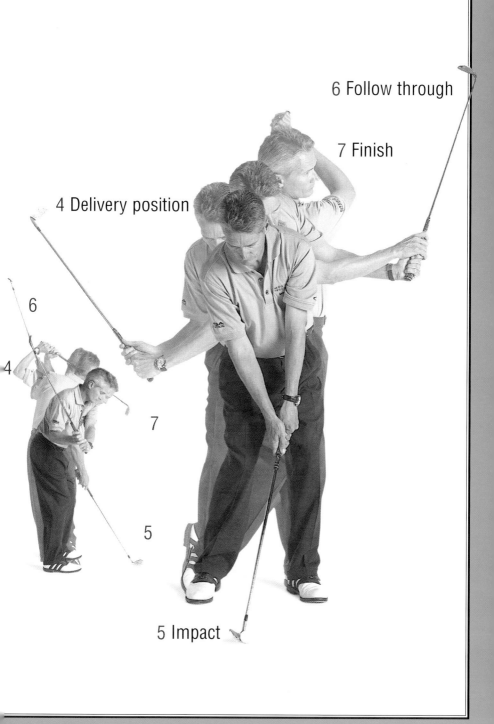

6 Follow through

7 Finish

4 Delivery position

6

4

7

5

5 Impact

Part Swing: Pitching

The difference between Pitching and Chipping

For many people, the difference between these two shots may be more of academic concern than anything else. For them, the two terms are used interchangeably. However, it is worthwhile considering that there are some differences centring on the trajectory of the shot, and the way it is played.

Generally, a pitch shot has a higher trajectory and doesn't roll as far. A chip shot is a low trajectory shot that gets off the ground for a short period and then rolls. When determining which shot to play, an old golfing adage should be borne in mind:

'Putt when you can, Chip when you can't putt and Pitch only when you have to.'

This saying supports my previous advice to consider using the putter even in some off-the-green situations, and indicates the difference in execution of chips and pitches. A pitch shot is used when the ball is in the rough, and/or when you need height on the shot but require the ball to stop after landing, and not to roll on. A chip is used when the ball is on the fringe of the green and you can't putt due to the condition of the grass between the ball and the hole.

Both pitch shots and chip shots can also be played as pitch-and-run, or chip-and-run shots where a club with less loft is used and the ball is played to run on after landing as conditions dictate.

Pitching

Pitching is a part swing. However, the pitching swing belongs to the full swing family. It is a two-lever swing, which means there is wrist action required to create the second lever of the club. The most important pitch shot to learn is the half swing or '9 o'clock back-swing'.

The rule that I like to employ for all part shots is 'set-up is impact'. This means that the position of your body, legs, arms and club in set-up exactly replicate the position they swing through at impact. 'If it doesn't need to move' in any part swing, 'it shouldn't'. Our goal is to

be able to be totally aware of the target and hitting the ball there. If you have to concentrate on making contact with the ball then this will distract from the consistent outcome of the shot. The more simple and uncomplicated we can make the pitching action, the better.

Like all golf swings, the pitching action is a blend of set-up, pivot, plane and position and dynamics. All are important to a good pitching game; however, the best pitchers all have great rhythm. Great rhythm means a smooth even-flowing swing that repeats to the same beat regardless of the shot being played.

Rhythm

I recommend the use of a metronome for all part shots. Musicians use a metronome to maintain and practise the rhythm of the music they are playing. I have found no better way of practising golf shots.

A golfer's rhythm will vary from player to player. However, most short shots work very well with a one-second beat between take-away and impact. Set the metronome to 60 beats per minute and visualise swinging back on one beat and making contact on the next. One, two, one, two, one, two.

Distance control

Once you have mastered the 9 o'clock swing with a one, two rhythm, the only variation required to hit your pitch shots shorter or longer will be the length of the back-swing. With your pitching wedge you may hit the ball 50 yards with the 9 o'clock swing. From there, hit some pitch shots with an 8 o'clock left arm swing but always maintain the one, two rhythm. These shots will probably fly about 40 yards and then if you try a 10 o'clock swing these will fly about 60 yards.

There is a lot of individual variation in part shots. The key is to find out what you need to do to control the distance of your pitch shots. This method I have described is the method I use and has been most successful with my students. There are other methods for pitching, but as a basis to build on, this method suits every player.

1

2

Set-up: 'Set-up is impact' – The set-up is the same as step 5 in the full swing. The hips should be slightly open to the target, two-thirds of your weight over the left knee, the right knee flexed towards the ball and the right heel slightly lifted off the ground (this encourages a down and through angle of attack through impact). The stance is the same as the short iron stance, with the ball position in the middle of the feet and the left foot turned out 45°. The left foot turned out encourages a turn through impact around a stable left leg.

Delivery position: 'The letter L at 9 o'clock' – Start the swing by turning the upper body. Immediately after the first move, hinge the wrists and fold the right elbow. When the left arm is parallel to the ground (the 9 o'clock position) the club shaft and left arm should form a right angle and from face-on create the letter L. Your weight should have shifted slightly to the right, to about 45-55% between left and right foot. From behind, the club shaft should be on plane with the butt end pointing to the inside quarter of the ball. The distance between your right wrist and sternum should be the same as it was in the set-up. This distance is the radius of the swing and if it remains constant you will make solid contact with the ball every time.

3

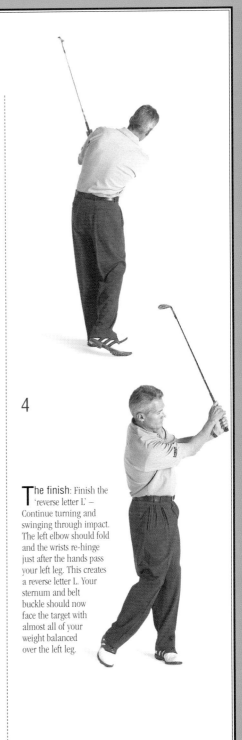

4

I mpact: 'Impact is set-up' – From step 2, focus on your right wrist staying in time with your sternum as you turn back to the set-up position. You always want the feeling of the arms and body working together in harmony, never independently of each other. At impact, the shaft is in line with the left arm, with the back of the left wrist facing the target and flat as it was in the set-up. The club is still travelling downward because of the ball position being back in the centre of the stance. Allow the loft of the club to do its job. No attempt should ever be made to lift or scoop the ball. A down and through impact is your aim. This imparts maximum back spin to the ball.

T he finish: Finish the 'reverse letter L' – Continue turning and swinging through impact. The left elbow should fold and the wrists re-hinge just after the hands pass your left leg. This creates a reverse letter L. Your sternum and belt buckle should now face the target with almost all of your weight balanced over the left leg.

Pitching Overview

2 Delivery position

2

1

1 Set-up

4 Finish

4

3

3 Impact

PART SWING: CHIPPING

THE BASIC CHIPPING STROKE

A chipping stroke is a one-lever stroke – an arm and shoulder swing dominated by the left arm with a firm wrist action. The basic chip shot does not include imparting a deliberate side-spin or back-spin. Practice must focus on getting the feel for distance through the length of the swing and correct club selection.

For this reason, different lies and ground course conditions must be experienced. Some golfers prefer to use just one club for all their chip shots. However the more clubs you become proficient with, the more shots you will have in your chipping arsenal and the better the 'fit' between what you can do and what is needed will become. Emphasis must again be on a square clubface at the point of impact with the ball, and consistent swing.

The actual chipping stroke itself is one in which the clubface 'brushes' the grass on the through swing: try to think of the ball being 'swept' away and allow the loft of the club to lift the ball more than anything else.

Club options range from the sand wedge through the 9, 8, 7 and 6 iron, as distance and conditions dictate. A 6 iron will run the furthest, the sand wedge (or lob wedge if you carry one) the shortest when both are used from the same spot.

You should check the grain of the green and the slopes involved before chipping, in order to determine the power of the stroke. Ball performance on the green should be noted for the reading of the green for the putt.

CHIPPING TECHNIQUE

The way the club is gripped is similar to the full swing technique, except the hands will be in a more neutral position with palms aligned to the clubface and facing each other. The single most important determining factor in clubface position is the grip.

Hands should be ahead of the ball to assist striking it with a slightly descending blow before brushing the turf. The extended line of the club shaft should point outside your left hip.

Many golfers prefer to grip down the handle to

get them closer to their work and to increase their control: this has the effect of shortening the length of the club. Whichever option you choose, the though, you must be consistent – you must grip all clubs at the same position/point for these shots so as to give sameness of feel on all occasions.

Note that by rotating the grip anti-clockwise, the right-handed golfer will increase the loft of the club and create higher, softer-landing shots; whereas rotating the grip clockwise decreases the loft and creates lower trajectory shots that release on landing and run towards the target.

Grip pressure on the club must not be changed throughout the stroke. Failure to maintain a constant pressure has adverse effects on timing, club control and speed.

CHIPPING SET-UP

Stance should be slightly open. Weight should be on the leading (target-side) foot. Ball position should be no further forward than middle of stance. Hands should be in front of the ball. Feet and body should be aimed 10°–20° left of target, enabling a free through-swing with firm wrists. The posture for chipping is essentially the same as for pitching. The main difference is that the body will be leaning more into the left side with the top of the backbone slightly on the target side of the ball. This set-up places most of the weight over the target-side knee, where it should stay throughout the stroke.

HOW TO PRACTISE CHIPPING

The sequence of practising is the same as for other aspects of the game: Set-up, Plane and Position, Pivot Motion and Dynamics (rhythm, timing, balance and tempo).

There are two types of chipping techniques:

- The putt-chip, where you use exactly the same technique as for your putting stroke: same grip, same stance with the only difference being that the ball is played back slightly to encourage a descending angle of attack at impact. You use a putting stroke to clip the ball away with the sole of the club just brushing the grass.

- Use an open stance and slight Pivot Motion on the way through.

The chipping swing is a one-lever action so you should have firm-wrists throughout. Upper arms are closely linked to the body. Your through swing should be as long, or slightly longer, than your back swing thus guaranteeing acceleration through the shot. The only moving parts of the body are on the through-swing when the right knee and the right hip will be allowed to turn slightly towards the target to permit a firm-wristed but free through-swing to the target.

Also, on the back swing, the arm and shoulder movement is confined to the shoulders 'rocking' around the axis of the upper spine. On the back stroke, move the target side shoulder down and on the through stroke shoulder up. Throughout the stroke the top of the backbone must stay perfectly centred. This is the only Pivot Motion.

1

2

3

4

CHIPPING OVERVIEW

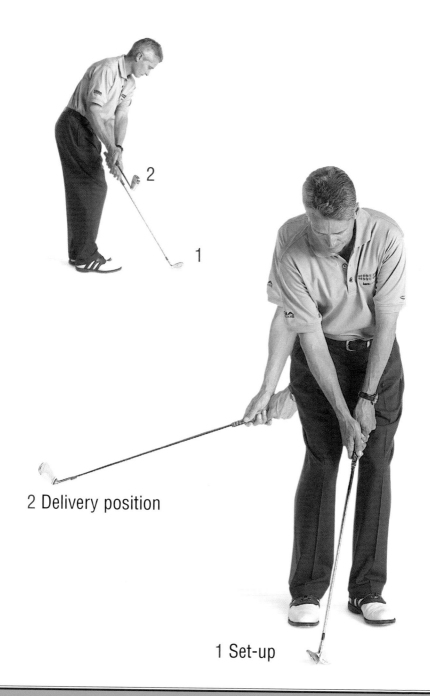

2 Delivery position

1 Set-up

4

3

4 Finish

3 Impact

PART SWING: BUNKERS

SAND SHOT TECHNIQUE

The standard bunker shot is the only shot where the club does not make contact with the ball. In this shot we are aiming to cut a slice of sand, about the size of a $20 note and about 1 inch thick, out from under the ball and onto the green.

Imagine the ball is sitting in the middle of this $20 note and gets a magic carpet ride on the sand out onto the green. The swing is a little bit longer on the back swing than it is with pitching swing (10 o'clock), to compensate for deliberately not making contact with the ball. The aim is to get the club head to 'skip' through the sand, not dig into the sand. To help achieve this, the clubface should remain open through impact by concentrating on contacting the sand with the trailing edge. This maintains the built-in bounce on the sole of the club.

If the clubface closes through impact the leading edge of the club will dig into the sand and will result in insufficient force to get the ball up and out of the bunker. A weakened grip (both hands rotated anti-clockwise on the grip) assists in keeping the clubface open.

The construction of the club – the sand wedge – with the back of the sole closer to the ground than its leading edge (bounce) makes it more likely that the clubface will actually skip through the sand.

In general, the length of the swing dictates the distance so it is important to maintain rhythm and tempo, and not to alter it (i.e. to hit harder or softer, to swing quicker or slower) to vary distance.

To vary the distance, vary the length of the swing, and as in pitch shots and chip shots, the follow-through should always be at least as long as the back swing.

There are two types of green-side bunker shots to be aware of:

- The first is the shot that we want to get up quickly, a high-lofted shot that will land near the pin and stop quickly. In this shot, your arms and the handle will stop at impact and allow the clubface to pass. 'Slow arms, quick club head' is a good key thought.

- A lower-trajectory bunker shot where the ball will release on landing and roll up towards the hole. This is usually a longer bunker shot covering some 25 to 30 metres (30 to 40 yards).

This second shot (a running bunker shot) is played with the arms moving through the shot so that the club head stays behind the handle. This creates less loft and less backspin due to the club head not travelling as fast under the ball. 'Slow club head, quick arms' is a good key thought.

THE BUNKER SET-UP

In all shots, a firm and balanced stance is critical. Nowhere is this more critical than for bunker shots. You should ensure you achieve this solid basis by working your feet soundly into the sand in the bunker. This involves twisting your feet/shoes well into the sand until foot movement is well and truly restrained.

If the target is at 12 o'clock, the clubface should be aimed at 1 o'clock and your toe line aimed at 11 o'clock.

Ball positioning should be 7cm forward of centre because you want to hit the sand the same distance behind the ball. I recommend you check that this positioning is correct as the altered, open stance with its deviated, left-oriented alignment has a tendency to make you feel that the ball is too far forward.

Your posture should be the same as for pitching, keeping in mind the 'set-up is impact' rule. Your upper body should be perpendicular to the sand.

HOW TO PRACTISE BUNKERS

The sequence of practising the mechanics of bunker shots is the same as for pitching and chipping. The pitching swing and the bunker swing are similar, except for the fact that the clubface is open in the normal bunker shot.

Allow the back of the left wrist to cup (creating an angle between the back of your hand and the back of your forearm) on the back swing thus opening the clubface more than in a normal swing. Also, at the point of impact when the club head 'splashes' through the sand, allow the club head to pass the handle (unlike pitch shots where the club shaft maintains alignment with the left arm). This presents maximum loft, maintains the bounce of the club and ensures that the club head splashes through the sand.

The plane is a little steeper on the back swing in order to get the clubface to penetrate into the sand, so the shaft may be slightly more vertical than normal. For consistent impact results it is imperative that the head stays at the same level throughout the entire swing.

1

2

3

4

Bunker Overview

2 Delivery position

2

1

1 Set-up

4 Finish

4

3

3 Impact

Putting

Technically, the putt should the easiest stroke to learn. The power requirements are minimal, and the motion requires no great dexterity. Why, then, is a player's putting often the weakest part of their game? From a technical viewpoint, most golfers don't think their putting stroke is worth practising. A few putts on the practice green before the round is all that is necessary. Unfortunately, good putting is a precise process. Not only do you need a good technique, but also the stroke has to be practised regularly. Enough of the lecture, let's proceed.

Three simple rules

I teach and use a putting stroke based on three simple rules:

- Set-up is impact: everything, including the putter face, shaft, hands, wrists, elbows and head are all set-up exactly where they need to be at impact.

- If it doesn't need to move, it shouldn't move: all unnecessary movement should be removed from the stroke. This includes body and head movement and the changing of angles at the wrist, elbow and shoulder joints.

- The dominant hand is the controlling hand: the hand that is used for all precise and detailed work (such as handwriting), must be the dominating and controlling hand of the stroke.

The Set-up

The following is a list of important geometric relationships. The references are to particular frames of the three putting sequences: putt-behind, putt-front and putt-target.

Your left eye should be over the ball, and your eye-line parallel to the target line. The width of stance can vary but must be stable and balanced. Grip through the palms with the hands placed proportionally on the handle. The shaft should be an extension of the forearms. The upper backbone is perpendicular to the plane of motion. The shaft should lean slightly toward the target.

This encourages solid contact, a clean take-away and firm wrist action.

The Stroke

The follow-through should be approximately twice as long as the back swing. This will guarantee that the putter head will be accelerating at impact. This reduces the tendency for the putter head to twist, sending the ball off-line. The angles between the forearm and the shaft remain constant throughout the stroke.

Similarly, your elbows, upper arms and shoulders maintain the same geometric relationships to each other. To achieve this, it is imperative that the shoulders rotate around the upper back on a plane that is parallel to that of the shaft and forearms at impact. If the shoulders don't rotate freely, it will be necessary to use the wrist, elbow or shoulder joints to move the putter back and through. This complicates the motion and causes inconsistency.

Tempo and rhythm

The stroke can be quick or slow but it must be rhythmical and work to a one, two musical-type beat. To control the length of the putt, shorten or lengthen the stroke. To get a feel for the rhythm and a speed that suits you, once again I recommend the use of a metronome. Start with a 72 beats per minute stroke. One beat on take away and one at impact. Good putters' rhythms range from 60 to 80 beats per minute. So some experimentation will be required until you find what suits you best.

Forearm rotation

No rotation of the forearms is demonstrated by the fact that the putter face is still perpendicular to the swing plane at the completion of the stroke.

Swing plane

With the shoulders rotating on a plane with the same angle as that defined by the forearms and shaft, the putter head will appear to move to the inside on the backstroke, return to on-line at impact, and move to the inside on the through stroke. The putter face should be perpendicular to the path at all times. A line drawn up the shaft and forearms and extended through the upper back should be perpendicular to the upper back.

NO HIT

A putt should be a stroke, not a hit. This is achieved by maintaining constant grip pressure throughout the stroke. In particular, awareness of the dominant hand controlling the stroke is imperative.

CONCLUSION

Putting needs to be treated as a precision activity. Attention to detail, especially the geometry of the set-up position, will pay dividends.

1

2

3

4

PUTTING OVERVIEW

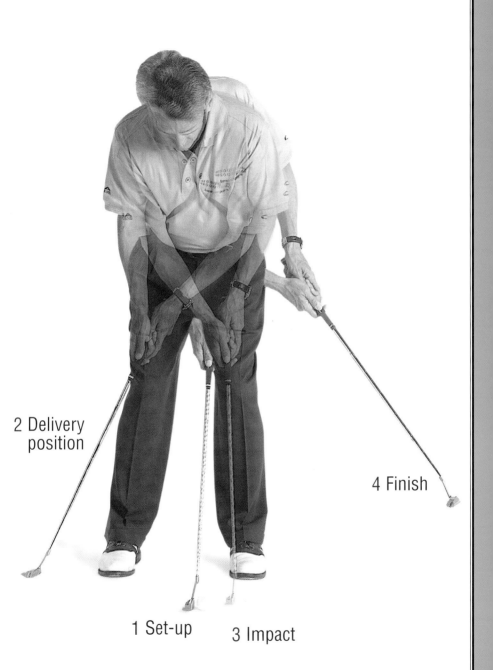

2 Delivery position

4 Finish

1 Set-up

3 Impact

Mental Skills

Mental skills in golf are of utmost importance to playing well. I believe the three most valuable elements of confidence, concentration and commitment will cover everything that is needed to play golf at your highest level.

Confidence is the most important of mental skills. Without confidence, it is almost impossible to consistently hit true and precise golf shots that lead to consistently good scoring. Positive confidence is almost always a direct consequence of preparation and experience. However, it is also a matter of choice. If the golfer chooses to focus on past failures, they will demonstrate 'negative confidence'. By recalling a past poor shot, they will recreate the physiology that caused that poor shot. The shot produced as a result of this process is likely to be an exact replica of the recalled poor shot.

Therefore, there is such a thing as negative confidence and this normally has a 100% success rate. If you think you are going to hit a bad shot, you almost certainly will. However positive confidence only has at best a 70% success rate. This is the nature of golf. The best players in the world only hit 7 out of 10 greens and fairways and only get the ball up and down when they miss the green 70% of the time. Golf can't be perfected, but you can be better and more consistent if you choose positive confidence.

Typically, what I see when a golfer is practising hitting 10 or 20 balls is that they take little notice of their good shots, because that is what they are expecting. And yet when they hit two or three poor shots there is often an emotional shift of frustration, anger or disappointment. So even though the ratio of good shots to bad shots was 7 to 3 in favour of the good shots, the shots that are stored in the long-term memory and easily recalled at a later date are the bad shots.

The key to positive confidence is to learn to anchor into your long-term memory the good shots in practice and play. The way to do this is to take notice of what it looks like, feels like and sounds like when you hit a good shot. Then give yourself a mental pat on the back and pump yourself up with a few positive affirmations. This creates a positive emotional shift and when you need to draw on some confidence from past experiences they are more likely to be positive as a result of this process. When you hit a bad shot, practise not becoming emotional about it. Just evaluate, adjust and learn from it and move on with as little an emotional shift as possible. This way the bad shot will not be anchored in your memory.

Concentration

Concentration is the ability to think and focus on a task or thought exclusive to any other distraction. A golf shot takes about 40 seconds. In this timeframe your concentration will go through three phases, starting with external concentration, then internal concentration and finally control concentration.

External concentration is the ability to focus on everything outside of you. The external things that we need to concentrate on to play golf well are the wind, the lie of the land, obstacles, target area and distance, including how the ball will react when it is on the ground, is the ground hard or soft, wet or dry and so on.

Internal concentration is the ability to monitor and control what is going on in your body; for example, muscle tension and energy levels. Awareness of where our body, limbs and club are placed without looking at them is a very important function. Internal concentration is the ability to pre-program the feel of the swing required for the upcoming shot.

Control concentration is the ability to focus and hold a thought. In golf when you hear players talking about committing to a shot, what they are saying is they were able to hold and commit to the swing that they pre-planned with external and internal concentration.

Daily One-Minute Concentration Drills

External: for 20 seconds, practise observing everything that you can see, hear and feel. Don't let your mind think of anything else except external thoughts.
Internal: for 20 seconds, think only about what you feel within your body. Muscle tension, your breathing, heart-beat, the feel of your arms and legs etc. and sense where they are in space without looking.
Control: for 20 seconds, pick up a golf ball and look at it and only think of the ball. The colour,

feel, logo, dimples etc. This is hard, but if you can control your focus on the ball for 20 seconds, you will have the concentration required to commit to any shot.

The concentration process of every shot starts with the external concentration of evaluating the distance, target area, wind, lie of the ball and whether the shot is uphill, downhill or flat. From this point, you will select a club and type of shot you intend playing and then move to the internal concentration of programming the feel and image of the swing. Finally, after setting-up to the ball with the shot ready to go, you move to control concentration by committing to the shot, and not letting your mind wander from the planned shot for the duration of the swing.

In between shots it is best to relax and enjoy the walk, scenery and the company of your playing partners. When it is your turn to hit a shot, the concentration process starts again.

Strategy

One shot at a time attitude

The essence of a 'one shot at a time attitude' is to always keep in mind where the next shot should be played from, but never how the next shot will be played.

The aim is to ensure that you do not get swamped by events or over-awed by what is going on around you. The proven and most effective way to play is called Procedure orientation (focusing only on the procedure of playing the shot at hand). Outcome orientation (focusing on the score, the result, what other people will think etc.) should be avoided at all cost.

This philosophy enables you to focus on the job at hand and effectively shut out anything irrelevant.

A golfer with this attitude will be thinking and focusing on the things they can control, effectively shutting out and over-riding the thoughts of the things they can't control.

Concentration is maximised, allowing you to call on all aspects of your practice that will assist in the situation at hand. It gives you permission to forgive yourself for any previous poor shots, wrong judgments and even simple bad luck.

Course management skills

Course management is another aspect of strategy and preparation. Confidence is the direct result of preparation. Course management is the ability to move the ball around the course in the way you want, in the least number of shots.

Utilise your handicap effectively. For example, if you have an 18 handicap you will only need to hit every hole in one more shot than regulation. This means on a par 4 you should hit the green in 3 shots and take 2 putts for a score of 5; less your handicap stroke, the result is a net 4. Is it then necessary to hit a driver off the tee and force a long iron in an attempt to hit the green? Often the result when you attempt this can end up being a double bogey 6 or worse. Think about a 3 or 5 wood off the tee, followed by a medium iron to the opening of the green, from where you can play a pitch or chip safely toward the pin and take 2 putts. Of course, on occasion you might only need 1 putt for a net birdie!

Course management means getting the most out of your game and playing to your ability based on your handicap, capability and the course in question. It is a course and strategy-focused preparation rather than a 'mechanics'-based preparation.

This focus is designed to enable you to play the course in question to your strengths, and not simply just 'play' a round. Therefore, club selection will be based on a mixture of what suits you, and the layout/requirements of the course itself.

For example, where the course comprises hard greens and heavy rough off the fairway, you may elect to include a 7 wood rather than a long iron to enable you to play a high long shot from the rough that will still stop on the green. Whereas on a course in an area that is windy with long par 4s and dry green surrounds you might elect to carry all your long irons, for long, low running shots.

For a course that includes deep bunkers or green side mounds and valleys, you may opt for a 3 wedge approach that includes a lob wedge with 60° or more of loft.

The primary aim is to get away from the 'Hit and Hope' approach to the game.

TRAFFIC LIGHT STRATEGY

One way of assessing the upcoming shot is to visualise each shot as fitting into one of three categories – red light, amber light or green light.

RED LIGHT SHOT

A red light shot is the shot to play when you have absolutely no other option. It is a desperation shot. It is played when you really have your back up against the wall. If it succeeds, then you are a hero. If it doesn't, you're a real idiot! You may consider a red light shot if the position is such that in match play you need to get back into the game. For example, you may need to hit the ball over water, against a strong left-to-right wind in order to land on the green and stay among the leaders.

The down-side of red light shots is that the 'penalty' (i.e. what happens to your score if you don't manage to pull the shot off) is a double bogey or worse. Whereas in match play, at worst it can only mean loss of a hole.

AMBER LIGHT SHOT

With an amber shot, the element of risk involved in the shot is less than for a red light shot. Amber shots are stepping up the aggression in search of birdies. You would be looking to produce an amber shot, for instance, when things were going fairly well, your confidence was up and you had the chance to make birdie or eagle with some aggressive golf. An example would be if the pin was on the front left of the green just over a bunker. If you shoot straight for the pin, and clear the trap, a short birdie putt is the result. If you fall short in the bunker you can still get it up and down and salvage par. If the shot fails, this amber light shot should not penalise you more than a bogey at worst (i.e. if the ball bounces through the green you can still get back on the green and save par or at worst bogey the hole).

GREEN LIGHT SHOT

These are the safest and most conservative shots to play. You hit the ball in the middle of the fairway, the middle of the green. Always setting up the biggest margin for error: long, short, left and right. Always lag the first putt into the one metre/one yard radius circle to guarantee the two putt. There is no real risk involved in your play. The down-side with this play is that there is less chance of making birdies. It is surprising, however, how many times the hole gets in the way when you are just trying to roll it up close with the correct speed. Many leading Tour Pros elect to play green light golf for the first few holes to set up the foundation of a good score.

It requires discipline to fire away from the pin to the middle of the green. It is important to hit an aggressive shot to a conservative target. Don't just fire away from the pin, pick a precise target and make a positive swing and shoot at the target. Many golfers fall into the trap of steering the ball when they try to play conservative golf.

STRATEGY SUMMARY

Within the overall philosophy of a 'one shot at a time attitude', golfers can elect to play a safe shot/game, or to engage in an attacking shot/game.

The decision is yours and your approach should change dependent on your confidence and the set-up of the course and your prepared game plan.

Some golfers prefer to play a round of golf in a cautious way, hitting safe, predictable shots off the tee and from the fairway and wait for the odd birdie to come their way.

This style in match play relies on your opponent making a mistake and letting you capitalise on it by virtue of your reliability.

In stroke play a Pro will make a living but have little chance of being in contention come Sunday if they don't play some aggressive golf.

Other golfers will play an attacking, amber or red light type game hoping to demoralise their opponent and blow them off the course by their audacious approach. In stroke play, they will finish their week high up and make big cheques, when it doesn't come off they will miss the cut.

You could argue the second approach for Pros is the best method. My philosophy is to work toward a blend of conservative and attacking golf and be able to manage the decision-making between the two.

The key to it all is that YOU are the one who decides the shot you will play.

CONCLUSION

My goal in this book was to create a reference for golfers of all levels that can be used to improve their game and can always be returned to when we recognise it is time to get back to basics. By now, you understand how golf can be learnt and improved through the process of the improvement cycle and that golf requires a holistic approach that involves more than just improving your swing.

To use a famous quote from Arnold Palmer on the essence of golf: 'Golf is deceptively simple and endlessly complicated. It satisfies the soul and frustrates the intellect. It is, at the same time, rewarding and maddening. It is without doubt the greatest game mankind has ever invented.'

It has been my experience that golfers who choose to have fun improve at a greater rate and their enjoyment of the game brings them back time and again to the course. So please, choose fun and remember that golf is a game and a privilege if we are lucky enough to have the opportunity to play.

GLOSSARY

Birdie: one shot less than par (3 shots on a par 4).

Bogey: one shot more than par (6 shots on a par 5).

Bunker shot: a shot played from the sand trap around the green.

Chipping: a shot that carries a short distance and then rolls to the hole.

Driver: the longest hitting club in the bag which is used from the teeing ground.

Down-Swing: the swing of the club down to the ball from the top of the back swing.

Fairway Shots: shots played from the mown grass between the tee and green.

Fairway Woods (Metals): a wooden or metal head long club used on the fairway.

Long Irons: the numbers 1,2,3 and 4 irons.

Mid Irons: the numbers 5,6,7 and 8 irons.

Par: the number of shots designated as a standard for playing a golf hole.

Pitching: less than a full swing shot that is lofted onto the green.

Putting: a shot that is used on the green that has no loft and rolls the ball.

Short Irons: the numbers 9, wedge and sand irons.

Steering: trying to over control the swing by not swinging freely through impact.

Swing Plane: the path that the club head traces in the swing (side view).

Tee Shots: shots played from the teeing area at the beginning of a hole.

About the Author

Steve Bann is one of Australia's best known golf coaches. After turning professional in 1979, he played on the Australian Professional Golf Tour from 1981 to 1996.

In the early '90s, Steve commenced golf instruction full-time as the founding Head Coach of the world-renowned Victorian Institute of Sport. He nurtured and developed the program, which has produced multiple international amateur and professional tournament winners. The VIS program is now considered the template approach to developing golfers and is followed by many of the World sporting Institutes.

In 1989, during Steve's tenure as Head Coach of the Victorian men's team, he began coaching the then-upcoming junior Stuart Appleby (five-time winner on the US Tour and 2001 Australian Open winner) and has coached Robert Allenby (four-time winner on the US Tour, four-time winner on the European tour and 1994 Australian Open champion) since Robert was 14 years old. He remains Stuart Appleby's coach to this day and travels regularly with him on the US PGA Tour.

Steve has a keen interest in golf history and improvement methods, particularly how computer technology and analysis can assist golfers to lower their scores. Steve also shares his knowledge of the game through his delivery of presentations and lectures to fellow golfers, both amateur and professional, including the 1992, 1994, 1996 and 2002 and 2004 Australian PGA golf summits.

Outside of golf, Steve's main interests are personal fitness, tennis and fishing. Steve originates from Riversdale Golf Club in Melbourne, where he was introduced to the game as a caddie and is today still a club member.